Our **WILD**™ **WORLD**
SERIES

Leopards

NorthWord Press
Minnetonka, Minnesota

DEDICATION
To Anthony Bodo, a friend and fellow reader

© NorthWord Press, 2002

Illustrations by John F. McGee
Designed by Russell S. Kuepper
Edited by Barbara K. Harold

NorthWord Press
5900 Green Oak Dr
Minnetonka, MN 55343
1-800-328-3895
www.northwordpress.com

Library of Congress Cataloging-in-Publication Data

Feeney, Kathy
    Leopards / Kathy Feeney ; illustrations by John F. McGee.
      p. cm. -- (Our wild world series)
    Summary: Describes the physical characteristics, behavior, and habitat of leopards.
    ISBN 1-55971-809-9 (hc.) -- ISBN 1-55971-796-3 (soft cover)
      1. Leopard--Juvenile literature. [1. Leopard.] I. McGee, John, ill. II. Title. III. Series.

QL737.C23 F39 2002
599.75'54--dc21   2001054609

Printed in Singapore

10 9 8 7 6 5 4 3 2 1

Our WILD™ WORLD SERIES

Leopards

Kathy Feeney
Illustrations by John F. McGee

NORTHWORD PRESS
Minnetonka, Minnesota

HAVE YOU EVER HEARD of a wild cat called "Prima Ballerina" or "Prince of Cats"? These are nicknames for the leopard. It is one of the world's six big cats, along with lions, tigers, cheetahs, cougars, and jaguars. They all are related, and they belong to the scientific classification, or group, called Felidae (FEE-lih-dee). This is the Latin word for "cat family."

The name leopard comes from the Latin words *leo*, which means lion, and *pard*, which means panther. Scientists use the Latin name *Panthera pardus*, or "the leopard panther." Most people usually shorten it to just "leopard."

Leopards have roamed the Earth since the days of the dinosaur. Scientists have identified leopard fossils that are two million years old. Today, leopards live in parts of Africa, the Middle East, India, China, Siberia, and southeast Asia.

Keen eyesight is one of the leopard's senses that helps it find food and stay alert for nearby enemies.

Young leopards soon learn to find a good place to rest or take a quick nap.

Leopards can adapt, or change, to live in many kinds of places, called their habitat. They always choose habitats that provide plenty of food and shelter. Leopards may be found in tropical rain forests, snowy mountains, jungles, and the wide-open grasslands called savannahs.

You may think it would be simple to see leopards in the wild. But their speckled coloring helps to camouflage (KAM-uh-flaj), or hide, them. Leopards blend into their surroundings and can become nearly invisible in the trees, rocks, and long grass where they live.

Leopards
FUNFACT:

Antarctica is the only place on Earth that has no members at all of the whole cat family.

To help protect themselves while getting a drink out in the open,
away from good camouflage, leopards stay low to the ground.

The snow leopard has an excellent breathing system. The very cold air is warmed through its nostrils before it goes into the lungs.

There are three types, or species (SPEE-sees), of leopards. They are the snow leopard, the clouded leopard, and the "true" leopard. Snow leopards are found in the mountains of central Asia. They have very large paws, or feet, which act like snowshoes to help them walk on top of the deep snow. When the winter becomes too harsh, snow leopards often move to lower land, where there are more trees for protection from the weather. They have long grayish coats, or fur, with scattered black spots and a long bushy tail. They sometimes use their tails to cover their faces for added insulation in cold temperatures.

Adult snow leopards measure up to 7 feet (2 meters) from nose to tail, and weigh up to 155 pounds (70 kilograms). Their light color helps them hide in the snow of their habitat.

Clouded leopards usually hunt from trees in the daylight. They often hunt on the ground beginning around sunset.

Clouded leopards live in the rain forests of southeast Asia. They are gray or yellow with black and brown spots. They also have some stripes on their heads. An adult is smaller than the other leopard species. It is about 6 feet (1.8 meters) long from nose to tail. Clouded leopards weigh between 35 and 55 pounds (16 and 25 kilograms).

They are named after their spot patterns, which look like groups of clouds. The clouded leopard is also known as the "mint leopard," because some people think its spots look like mint leaves. These same markings help clouded leopards disappear into the tree branches, where they spend much of their time. This is the species most likely to hunt from trees, and ambush an animal on the ground below.

The "true" leopard is the one that most people recognize. This species is found in the wild from South Africa to east of Russia. Adult male leopards are usually 7 feet (2 meters) long from their noses to their tails. They can weigh from 150 to 200 pounds (68 to 90 kilograms). A full-grown female averages 5 feet (1.5 meters) in length and weighs from 80 to 150 pounds (36 to 68 kilograms). Females of all the leopard species are usually smaller than the males.

Depending on the species, a leopard's coat may be a different color, from grayish to pale yellow to tan to gold. But all leopards have spots. Each animal has its own unique spot pattern, just as every human has his or her own unique fingerprints. These spot patterns are often used by scientists who study animals, called zoologists (zoe-OL-uh-jists), to identify individual leopards.

Leopards have good balance, even on slippery rocks crossing a stream. Their tails help them keep their balance.

Some people mistake leopards for cheetahs or jaguars. All three of these cats are nicknamed "the sports cars of cats," because they are sleek, swift, and spotted. But once you compare them side-by-side, it's easy to tell them apart by their spots.

The cheetah has solid black spots that look like polka dots all over its body. The spots on leopards and jaguars are grouped in circles. These markings are called rosettes, because they look like rings of blooming roses. To tell the difference between these two animals, just look at the color in the center of the rosette. Jaguars have rosettes with brownish hair in the center and a black spot. The middle of a leopard's rosette is just plain, brownish hair.

The leopard's fur is thick and soft. Its head and legs have solid black spots. Its undercoat, or belly, is pure white. Leopards have a long spotted tail with a white tip.

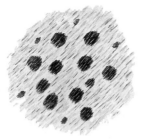

Cheetah

Jaguar

Leopard

If an enemy approaches, such as this hyena, a leopard may quickly
jump up into a tree, where its spots still work like camouflage.

A black leopard may have an advantage in hunting because its dark color acts as better camouflage in the low-light conditions of its home in the rain forest.

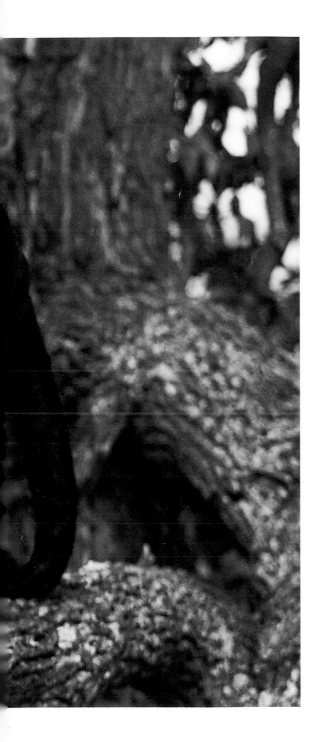

Some leopards are pure black. They are called panthers. But they are not a separate species. Even though their spots are difficult to see, they do have them. These black leopards can be born into a litter, or group, of babies that also has members with gold, beige, or gray coats. They grow up just like their siblings, or brothers and sisters. The only difference between them is their coat color.

Leopards
FUNFACT:

A leopard is 10 times stronger than a human of the same weight. Its sense of hearing is approximately two times stronger than a human's hearing.

A mother and her young sometimes find good resting places in the same tree.

The size, weight, and coat color of a leopard also depends on where the animal lives. Light-colored leopards usually live in grassland regions with a few clumps of trees. Leopards found in the desert are sandy colors, such as cream and yellowish brown. Golden-colored leopards live in forest habitats and use the tree shadows to help camouflage themselves. Panthers usually live in jungles where their black coats help them disappear into dark shadows.

Leopards have strong, thick necks and faces with high cheekbones and golden, oval-shaped eyes. Their ears are rounded and their noses are long and wide.

Leopards have broad chests and powerful, short legs for animals of their size. They can run in short sprints up to 37 miles (60 kilometers) per hour.

Leopards also climb trees, where they hide, rest, sleep, and store their food. They often spend time in trees to avoid the insect pests that may be in the grass below. If a leopard feels threatened by a predator, or enemy, it will usually run away or escape to safety up a tree, rather than fight.

These leopard babies already look like their mother, and will grow quickly and soon be as large she is.

Leopards can move very quickly when they are hunting for food.
And they have good concentration to secretly follow their prey.

Like all members of the cat family, leopards seem to be walking on their tiptoes. This is called digitigrade walking. Leopards actually walk on soft, cushioning pads underneath their toes and on the soles of their paws. They have five toes on their front paws and four toes on their back paws. The pads are surrounded by short, thick fur that helps the leopard keep its balance on slippery rocks and in trees. Both the pads and this extra fur also help the leopard travel silently to surprise the animals they hunt for food, called prey (PRAY).

This leopard is leaving a message for other leopards, "Stay away! This is my home."

Just like one of its other relatives, the house cat, leopards have needle-sharp, curved claws, which they can retract, or pull back, into their paws. The leopard's claws are about 1 inch (2.5 centimeters) long. They are usually retracted to protect them from wearing down or becoming injured. Leopards keep their claws sharp by scratching them on rough surfaces such as tree trunks. Claws are used as weapons for fighting, and as tools for catching and holding prey. They are also used to communicate messages to other leopards by scratching marks on tree trunks.

Leopards are nocturnal (NOK-turn-ul) animals, which means they are more active at night. That is when they travel, hunt, and feed. They are rarely seen in daylight hours. During the day they usually sleep in trees or bushes to keep cool and safely hidden. They may also sun themselves on rocks and sometimes eat the meat from an earlier hunt.

If a leopard senses danger nearby, it may try to scare the enemy away by looking ferocious and showing its teeth.

Leopards have excellent senses of hearing, sight, and smell. They have the best night vision of the six big cats and can locate their prey in almost complete darkness. A leopard's vision may be as much as seven times better than a human's eyesight.

The leopard can see so well in the dark because it has reflective, or mirror-like, layers at the back of its eyes. In bright light, the leopard's pupils become narrow slits. The pupil is the black circle in the center of each eyeball. In dark surroundings the pupils open wide to let in the most light possible. This is when the leopard's eyes appear to glow in the dark.

This leopard is carefully watching and listening to something in the distance.
Its whiskers will move depending on whether it feels safe or threatened.

The leopard's long, white whiskers are stiff, sensitive hairs that help it feel its way in the dark. Like other members of the cat family, leopards have whiskers, called vibrissae (vie-BRISS-ee), in three separate places on the head. Some whiskers grow above the eyes. Some are located behind the leopard's cheeks. And very long whiskers grow on each side of the muzzle, at the front.

A leopard's vibrissae can point in different directions, depending on how the animal is feeling and what it is doing.

When leopards are at rest, their whiskers point sideways. When excited or threatened, their whiskers stick upward. When they are hunting and traveling, their whiskers spread out and fall forward in the shape of a fan. This position allows the whiskers to work like radar so the leopard can avoid bumping into things in the dark. The whiskers help tell the leopard the best spot on its prey to make a deadly bite. The whiskers sense when the prey's nerves have stopped twitching and the animal is dead.

The leopard's thin, dark tail may be up to 3 feet (0.9 meter) long. That's longer than your whole arm. Sometimes, the tail is just as long as the whole rest of the leopard's body. The leopard swishes its tail before it leaps or runs. This back and forth movement helps the leopard keep its balance. A female leopard also uses her tail as a flag that her babies, or cubs, can follow when they travel.

The leopard is an excellent swimmer. But it does not spend time in water to cool off. Leopards usually visit a watering hole for a daily drink, even though they can live without water for as long as a month. Leopards do not need to drink often because they get liquids from eating prey.

Leopards are carnivores (KAR-nuh-vorz), or meat-eaters. But they are not picky about their food. The leopard's diet includes many creatures, from tiny insects to large mammals. The menu may include beetles, ostriches, porcupines, rodents, and reptiles. Antelope, deer, jackals, monkeys, and young zebras and cheetahs are also favorite prey animals.

Leopards also eat fish and some fruit. And they are scavengers (SKAV-en-jers), often feeding on carrion (KARE-ee-un), which are animals that are already dead.

Leopards
FUNFACT:

To stay healthy, females should eat approximately 6 pounds (2.7 kilograms) of meat every day. Males require nearly 8 pounds (3.6 kilograms) per day.

Sometimes a cub's curiosity makes it explore new things.
The turtle inside this shell is probably safe.

Before long, these young leopards from the same litter will separate to hunt and live on their own.

While cubs are still young, their mothers groom them.
They will soon learn to clean themselves.

Leopards have powerful jaw muscles and 32 teeth for crushing bones and tearing flesh. They use their teeth as weapons to grab onto the neck or head of their prey and then snap the animal's spine. Four canine teeth, which are 2 inches (5 centimeters) long, are used for biting and piercing. Curved and pointed like fangs, these teeth work like scissors to cut off pieces of meat, which are swallowed whole without chewing. A leopard can rip off its prey's fur by using its upper and lower front teeth, called incisors.

The leopard's tongue is rough and covered with hook-shaped spikes called papillae (puh-PILL-uh). These sharp bristles can be used by the leopard to scrape flesh from the bones of its prey. The tongue's papillae also come in handy for grooming, or cleaning, the leopard's fur. The mother grooms her babies often to keep them clean. This is very important so the cubs do not attract enemies by their scent, or odor.

Leopards silently stalk, or hunt, their prey. They stay hidden by lying flat on the ground and slowly creeping forward, sneaking up on their prey. When the leopard is about 15 feet (4.5 meters) away, it springs forward and pounces, or jumps, on the animal. Leopards sometimes wait patiently at waterholes for prey animals. They also follow the prey's tracks on the ground. Or the leopard pounces on prey from a hiding place high up in a tree. Leopards usually choose to attack young, sick, or older animals that are easier to catch.

Leopards
FUNFACT:

Many legends tell tales of the intelligence and cunning of the leopard. One says that to hide its tracks from predators, the leopard uses its tail to brush away its pawprints in the dirt or sand.

Leopards do not catch every prey animal they stalk and chase.
This gazelle is very fast and may escape.

If the kill is large, such as this warthog, the leopard must use all its strength to drag the prey up a tree to safety.

After each kill the leopard rips open the belly of its prey to remove the stomach and intestines. The leopard covers these organs with dirt, and eats the liver, kidney, and heart of its prey first. Then it eats the meat. Male leopards can go about three days without eating. Females with cubs need to eat nearly every day.

After feasting, a leopard drags the remains of the animal by the neck and pulls it high up into a tree. Leopards have been seen dragging 150-pound (68-kilogram) carcasses up trees that are as tall as two-story buildings.

The leopard hangs its prey over tree branches so the food won't be stolen by other animals looking for a meal. These scavengers include lions, hyenas, and vultures. The leopard can then safely leave, and return whenever it needs a meal. In desert habitats, leopards hide their food among rocks.

Their fierce hunting ability has given leopards a ferocious reputation. But they are really shy and peaceful mammals. Leopards are solitary, which means they prefer to live alone.

Leopards most often try to hide from their enemies, such as baboons, lions, tigers, and hyenas.

Leopards are also quiet animals. They don't make many vocalizations (vo-kul-ize-A-shuns), or sounds. Once in a while they cough, grunt, or can let out a low purr that sounds like a person sawing wood. Females let males know they are ready to mate by making loud growls. Leopard cubs make meowing sounds to call to their mother.

Male and female leopards are both territorial, which means they fiercely protect their territory, or home range. Depending on the food available, males may claim a home range as large as 11 square miles (30 square kilometers). That's about the size of a small town. Females usually live in smaller ranges that overlap with several other females' areas.

Male territories often overlap several female territories without problems. But if two male leopards try to live in one home range, they will probably fight. The loser of the fight must leave the area.

Leopards warn other animals to stay out of their territory by scent marking. Leopards do this by spraying their urine on trees, plants, and rocks. They also claw trees to make "keep out" or "no trespassing" signs.

Leaving scat, or droppings, is another way the animals claim their territory. Also, a male leopard can smell these signs and know if a female is ready to mate.

This leopard has just sprayed a tree trunk.
It will move on to mark other trees in its territory.

This cub is old enough to begin exploring outside the den. Its first journey will be with its mother, and not far from the den.

Unlike many other animals, leopards do not have one special time to breed. They mate year-round. Males become ready to mate around age three. Females are ready at age two. Female leopards usually give birth every two years.

After mating, a male and female go their separate ways. The male returns to his territory, leaving the female with the responsibility to raise and teach their offspring how to hunt for prey and survive in the wild.

The female leopard soon begins to prepare a den for her young in a cave, a hollow tree, or a thicket of plants. The cubs are born about three months later.

Female leopards usually have one to three cubs in a litter. Newborn leopards weigh about 1.5 pounds (680 grams). The cubs do not leave the den during their first two months. And their mother leaves them only for short periods of time to find food for herself.

Cubs need lots of rest to grow strong. They stay close to their mother for warmth, protection, and food.

As they grow, the cubs become playful and curious. Sometimes they try to explore on their own beyond the den. The mother leopard works hard to keep her babies safe from predators. If she senses danger, she carries them by the scruff of their neck, one by one, to a new hiding place. The leopard cub's enemies include adult male leopards, lions, tigers, pythons, baboons, and hyenas. The first year of life is a very dangerous time for the cubs, and they must learn quickly how to stay safe. About half of the leopard cubs that are born each year do not survive to become adults.

Leopard cubs are born with very woolly coats. At birth, their teeth are already starting to push through their gums. They are born with their eyes closed, but at about 14 days old, they open their eyes, which are light blue.

Mother leopards must have patience with young cubs as they play.
Sometimes their jumping games are rough and fast.

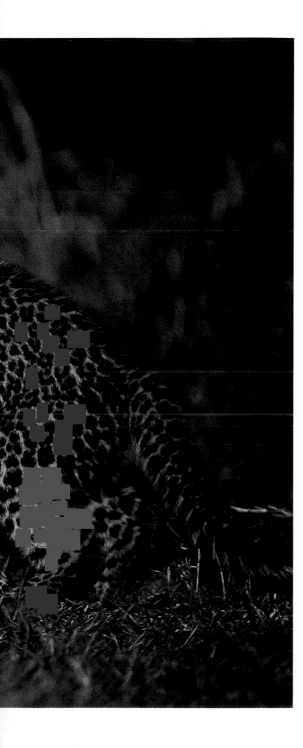

The babies drink their mother's milk until they are nearly six weeks old. Then their mother begins feeding them regurgitated, or chewed and spit out, pieces of meat.

By the time they are four months old, the young leopards look like miniature versions of their mother. Their eyes have turned golden and their coats are short, shiny, and spotted. By six months old, the young leopards learn how to hunt. Their mother teaches them where to find prey and how to climb trees. These are difficult things to learn and the cubs must practice many times. Sometimes they try their new skills by stalking and pouncing on each other.

Leopards
FUNFACT:

Even leopards take "catnaps" during the day when they get tired.

For a few more months, leopard cubs play by hunting mice and insects, but they mostly share their mother's meals. When they are nearly a year old their mother allows them to kill their own prey on a real hunt.

Female leopards hold their tails upright, high in the air, when they are traveling with their cubs. The cubs usually follow behind the mother in a single-file line. The young leopards can keep track of their mother by watching the white tip of her tail as they move around.

Young leopards live with their mothers for nearly two years before leaving to be on their own. Even then, siblings sometimes stay together for several more months before separating to claim their own territories. Sometimes females choose territories near their mother's home range. Young males usually travel farther away from where they were born.

Leopards can live to be 10 to 15 years old in the wild. Many things can affect their lifespan. Leopards can die from starvation and natural disasters, such as floods and forest fires. Some are also killed by other animals including hyenas and lions.

This cub needed some help getting back to the den. It doesn't hurt it to travel this way.

This snow leopard is using its strong leg muscles to run and jump over the snow. Its whole body is stretched out to cover more ground.

Climbing trees is as easy for leopards as walking on the ground.
High up on a narrow limb is a safe place to relax.

Humans are among the leopard's top enemies. Although the leopard is a protected species and it is illegal to kill them for their fur, thousands of the animals are still hunted each year by poachers. In some countries, claws and whiskers are made into potions and medicine.

Leopards need plenty of open space to roam and hunt. But they often lose their natural habitats when humans build homes in the leopard's territory.

Leopards in the southern half of Africa are a threatened species. This means their population is being closely studied. All other leopards in the wild are endangered, which means they are near to becoming extinct, or gone forever.

Through research, people who want to protect wildlife, called conservationists, gather information that will help leopards. Then they provide the information to others so they can learn new things about this secretive mammal. With the help of these caring humans, leopards will survive in the wild for many years to come.

Leopards
FUNFACT:

**Scientists say the leopard
is the most widely distributed
of the six big cats.
The worldwide population
is estimated to be about
600,000 in the wild.**

Internet Sites

You can find out more interesting information about leopards and lots of other wildlife by visiting these web sites.

www.africat.org	The AfriCat Foundation
www.animaldiscovery.com	Discovery Channel Online
www.dspace.dial.pipex.com/agarman/bco/ver4.htm	Big Cats Online
www.EnchantedLearning.com	Enchanted Learning
www.kidsplanet.org	Defenders of Wildlife
www.nationalgeographic.com	National Geographic Society
www.nwf.org	National Wildlife Federation
www.pbs.org/wgbh/nova/leopards	NOVA online/Leopards
www.snowleopard.org	International Snow Leopard Trust
www.tnc.org	The Nature Conservatory
www.wcs.org	Wildlife Conservation Society
www.worldwildlife.org/fun/kids.cfm	World Wildlife Fund

Index

Camouflage, 6, 7, 13, 14
Carnivore, 24
Claws, 20, 45
Clouded leopard (*Neofelis nebulosa*), 8, 9
Coat, 8, 10, 12, 15, 16, 37, 39, 40
Cubs, 24, 25, 28, 33, 36, 37, 38, 39, 40, 41

Den, 24, 36, 41

Ears, 15, 16, 21
Eyes, 5, 16, 18, 21, 27, 23, 36, 37, 39, 40

Food, 5, 6, 16, 24, 32, 33
Fur, 8, 12, 29, 45

Grooming, 28, 29

Habitat, 6, 8, 33, 45
Hunting, 9, 18, 23, 30, 36, 39

Leopard, "true," (*Panthera pardus*), 8, 10
Litter, 15, 36

Mating, 34, 36
Muzzle, 23
Nose, 16, 21

Panther, 14, 15, 16
Paws, 8, 19, 30
Predators, 16, 30, 37
Prey, 18, 19, 23, 24, 29, 30, 31, 39, 40

Size, 8, 9, 10, 16, 24
Snow leopard (*Uncia uncia*), 8, 43
Speed, 16
Spots, 8, 9, 10, 12, 15, 39
Stalking, 30, 31, 39

Tail, 8, 11, 12, 24, 30, 40
Teeth, 21, 29, 37
Territory, 34, 35, 41
Tongue, 29

Vocalizations, 33

Weight, 8, 9, 10, 15, 16, 36
Whiskers, 22, 23, 45

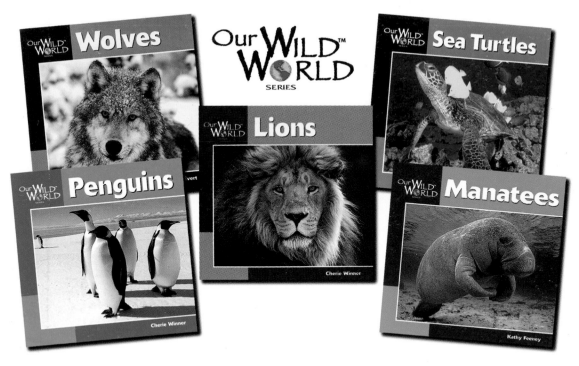

Paperback titles available in the Our Wild World Series:

BISON
ISBN 1-55971-775-0

BLACK BEARS
ISBN 1-55971-742-4

CARIBOU
ISBN 1-55971-812-9

COUGARS
ISBN 1-55971-788-2

DOLPHINS
ISBN 1-55971-776-9

EAGLES
ISBN 1-55971-777-7

LEOPARDS
ISBN 1-55971-796-3

LIONS
ISBN 1-55971-787-4

MANATEES
ISBN 1-55971-778-5

MOOSE
ISBN 1-55971-744-0

PENGUINS
ISBN 1-55971-810-2

SEA TURTLES
ISBN 1-55971-746-7

SHARKS
ISBN 1-55971-779-3

TIGERS
ISBN 1-55971-797-1

WHALES
ISBN 1-55971-780-7

WHITETAIL DEER
ISBN 1-55971-743-2

WOLVES
ISBN 1-55971-748-3

See your nearest bookseller, or order by phone 1-800-328-3895

NORTHWORD PRESS
Minnetonka, Minnesota
www.northwordpress.com